From Stories to Solutions

Redefining Communication Between Business and Data Professionals

Remco Broekmans

Technics Publications

SEDONA, ARIZONA

115 Linda Vista, Sedona, AZ 86336 USA

https://www.TechnicsPub.com

Edited by Sadie Hoberman
Cover design by Tirza Broekmans
Cartoons by Marco Wobben

All rights reserved. No part of this book may be reproduced or transmitted in any form or by any means, electronic or mechanical, including photocopying, recording or by any information storage and retrieval system, without written permission from the publisher, except for brief quotations in a review.

The authors and publisher have taken care in the preparation of this book but make no expressed or implied warranty of any kind and assume no responsibility for errors or omissions. No liability is assumed for incidental or consequential damages in connection with or arising out of the use of the information or programs contained herein.

All trade and product names are trademarks, registered trademarks, or service marks of their respective companies and are the property of their respective holders and should be treated as such.

Without in any way limiting the author's exclusive rights under copyright, any use of this publication to "train" generative artificial intelligence (AI) technologies to generate text is expressly prohibited. The author reserves all rights to license uses of this work for generative AI training and the development of machine learning language models.

First Printing 2025

Copyright © 2025 by Remco Broekmans

ISBN, print ed.	9781634626910
ISBN, Kindle ed.	9781634626927
ISBN, PDF ed.	9781634626934

Library of Congress Control Number: 2025931549

Contents

For Myrthe, Tirza, and Padmé

Acknowledgment

I never thought I would write a book and without the support I got, I would have probably never done this. It was quite a journey, and I am so thankful to have had many people who followed me along that path for a shorter or longer stroll.

First of all, I am grateful for the support from my wife and daughters throughout the process. Without their love, patience, and belief, I might have stopped somewhere along the path. On top of their support, they are also responsible for the artwork on the cover and the readable whiteboard art within the book. I could never thank them enough.

Special thanks to my friend, mentor, and business partner Hans Hultgren. He helped me in many phases of my data career and gave valuable feedback on my writing.

Thanks to Marco Wobben for his brilliant cartoons and for taking the time to discuss data modeling topics and support the ELM approach.

Also, thanks to Michael Müller for our coffee moments and his willingness to be Mr. Willibald.

Many thanks also go out to Steve Hoberman, not only my publisher but also a great supporter of writing down my knowledge into this book.

And, of course, thanks to the members of the DVEE Consortium for their critical thinking during the development of the ELM approach. Without that support and their criticism, the ELM approach wouldn't have been this strong.

A last thanks to everyone who participated in ELM workshops, attended the Business Mapping and ELM Certification training, responded to my LinkedIn posts, and attended my presentations anywhere in the world. Their remarks and questions gave me the extra push I needed.

Foreword

The classic divide between business and technical resources within organizations continues to create challenges for our enterprise data initiatives. The main symptom is a lack of communication, resulting in a compromised solution or outright failure. In addressing this chasm, this book outlines a realistic and viable path to align resources and facilitate clear communication.

From Data Vault modeling to the broader pattern of Ensemble Modeling, data warehouse deployments are becoming increasingly agile. At the same time, improving the connections to business resources is the main goal of our efforts at Genesee Academy and our consortium.

What you hold in your hands is a well-crafted manual that provides the methods and tools for closing the gap between business and technical resources. Remco Broekman's clear explanations, well-documented templates, and practical examples will guide you to successful workshops with fluid and productive communications.

Whether you're a business analyst, data analyst, project manager, IT manager, enterprise architect, or any data consumer, this book will empower you to communicate effectively with all stakeholders in your organization.

As you turn these pages, I trust that you will find the knowledge and inspiration needed to drive successful enterprise data initiatives in your organization.

Hans Patrik Hultgren
President Genesee Academy, LLC
January 2025

Introduction

When I first set foot in the data modeling jungle, it was unclear what to capture from all the available information. And for sure, it was not what I needed to provide to the business side of an organization. I listened to the stories in the organizations, did interviews, read business cases, and started making notes of the words and parts that I thought were important. Then, I looked around at what was available and started building a data model that I hoped would answer all the organizations' questions. I felt I could do it more efficiently, and I observed my peers and predecessors doing the same stuff and struggling as much as I did. I felt like I was in the movie Jumanji, where the team is solving the assignments by merely trying, after which a new part on the map appears with the next assignment. Step by step, this leads toward the end goal. I think it would have been done more efficiently with more guidance instead of just trial and error.

I do know I could have done with more assistance and guidance at some points. This is one of the reasons why I joined Hans Hultgren in further developing the ELM approach and its artifacts. Another reason was that I saw a clear miscommunication (if there was any form of communication at all) between the business and the IT sides. Not having an IT background when I started to work in the data field (25+ years ago) and have had numerous jobs in different organizations and many different roles, I got the feeling a lot was missing here. Communication, if there was any, seemed to be taking place in two completely different languages, where only some words sound familiar. The business context and background of the people involved are very important to understand to determine the actual meaning. This reality implies that we need communication beyond the status quo.

In some cases, there were efforts to convince the other side to use terms in their language (do the terms "Involved Party" or "OrderLine" ring a bell?), which really didn't help.

Clearly, the lack of communication and misunderstanding wasn't very helpful. And looking for AI assistance? I doubt if that will be able to bridge this gap on its own as it is learning from the past when we did not communicate. With the artifacts we came up with, the ELM approach is the first guidance to bridge this communication gap.

ELM makes it possible to translate the business story into an IT model without getting lost in translation.

I see this as a game where we investigate an area and do assignments and puzzles that need to be solved after a short story or sentence. Going from task to task and discovering the tile you are on, where the paths are revealed after each challenge. After mapping the whole tile, you move to the next tile and start discovering that one, step by step.

I wrote this book with my own experience and stayed away from heavy technical terms and jargon. I hope you enjoy reading the book, and it may also provide you with guidance.

CHAPTER ONE

Mapping the Business

This book is not about data modeling!

This book is about capturing stories, communication, and conversation.

This is not a book about storytelling, either!

This book will guide you on using stories to decide which road an organization needs to take, what information is important, and how to know.

For business-oriented people, this book will help you understand what IT needs to do to capture your ideas, needs, and requirements without being forced to understand their technical challenges and jargon. You can just communicate in your own words, and you will guide IT towards a solution that helps you to drive your organization. The IT side has a different way of communicating, and the challenge is to respect that and understand that they need to take more and smaller steps than you are used to. However, the benefit is a model understood by both sides of the organization, a clearer story, and better communication. The small steps mean you don't lose the IT side on your road. We need to walk the path together.

For IT-oriented people, communication with the business side of the organization might feel and sound unclear and incoherent. Try to move past the black and white, the bits and bytes, abstraction, and generalization. The business side has a different way of communicating, and the challenge is to respect that and understand that using different terminology doesn't mean using an invalid or incomplete data model. It might take more and smaller steps than you are used to. However, the benefit is a model understood by both sides of the organization, a clearer story, and better communication. The small steps mean you don't lose the business side on your road. We need to walk the path together.

This book hopefully guides both sides of the organization. Remember, there are two sides to a coin, it takes two to tango, etc. In other words, make an effort to understand the other side of the organization. They are not your opponents but a friendly and useful resource to fill in the gaps you miss from your end of the organization. The only way to bridge that gap is through communication, and the ELM approach is hopefully the guide that will encourage that communication.

Whenever you read the term data modeling in this book, it is a result of the combined effort of business and IT to map all the information and data that are important for any organization.

The ELM approach is all about communication with the business, or more specifically, the people running the day-to-day business, and can explain what is going on in the organization. This communication is essential for acceptance and commitment. At the same time, this is most likely not a smooth path to follow. In the ELM approach, we use the ELM artifacts as small tasks to discover that path to fully map a domain/subject area/business function in the organization. See this as the tile in the game, which is slowly being revealed.

The physical result of the ELM approach is the Ensemble Logical Model, which is used for communication (together with the ELM Artifacts). Or a fully mapped tile. This helps:

- **Business representatives**: To represent their own business, using their terminology and business concepts.

- **Data analysts/data stewards**: To understand and recognize the terminology, relations, and definitions/descriptions.

- **Source systems**: Through mapping, identify the needed information (Core Business Concepts, Relations, and Attribution) available in the source systems.

- **Developers/data engineers**: An almost one-to-one translation towards the desired Ensemble Modeling pattern (Data Vault, Anchor, Focal, etc.).

The resulting Ensemble Logical Model is an enterprise-wide business model that maps a given organization's business concepts. The ELM Artifacts is a guide towards a full logical model without losing the agility and adaptability needed when working with the business and their needs for data and information. Each tile connects to another tile and, as such, will provide a full map of the organization.

The picture in Figure 1 is not to scare you away and stop you from reading the book—it is merely the end result of mapping one domain/subject area/business function.

Figure 1: Example ELM.

The color coding and different shape styles in the model help in the translation:

- A blue (squared) box is the identifier (instance) of the Core Business Concept: Hub, Anchor, or Focal.

- A green (diamond-shaped) box is the unique, specific Natural Business Relation: Link or Tie.

- A yellow (round-edged) shape is the attribution and context describing the Core Business Concept: Satellite, Attribute, or Descriptor.

The Ensemble Logical model is the input for a technical implementation into any of the Ensemble Modeling patterns, such as Data Vault, Anchor Modeling, and Focal.

CHAPTER TWO

For Both Sides of the Organization

The Business Side

To make sense of the data in any organization, people on the IT side need to logically and physically model that data. That is, draw a map of the data side to provide you with the desired information. The terms they use for the resulting models are conceptual data models, logical data models, and physical data models. You will probably hear the following terms describing the modeling patterns: ERD schema, relational, 3NF, dimensional, star schema, Ensemble, Data Vault, Focal, Anchor model, etc. Basically, you can forget about all these terms.

> *The most important thing you can do to help the organization is to tell IT, in your own terminology, what you work with, what is important for you, what you need to know about, and how these terms are related.*

Using the ELM approach, any organization should be able to communicate both sides of the story: the business side and the IT side.

As IT is using your terminology in their modeling, you will be able to understand that model and help them improve it. Successfully expanding your future business needs requires these models and this shared understanding.

The IT Side

To create a data model, the people on the IT side of the organization need to make sense of the terms used in any organization and align these with the entities and data in the source systems. That is, create the conceptual, logical, and physical data model. It becomes hard to align source entities to the business terms when the sources use generic names or are abstracted, including roles and types. It would also be great if the business side of the organization was clearer in its wording and did not use multiple different terms for the same thing. Unfortunately, that is a reality the IT side of the organization needs to face, especially since the model should work for the entire organization (and minimize model changes). Basically, the reason for more generic modeling (using types and roles) is that it makes it more flexible and minimizes changes to the data model itself. Unfortunately, this also means that generic business terms make communication with the business more difficult. How can IT explain the importance of the generic term (with appropriate roles and types) if the business uses its own terminology? Using the ELM approach, any organization should be able to communicate both sides of the story: the business side and the IT side.

Note again that if IT is using business terminology in their modeling, IT will be able to discuss that model with the people on the business side. These same people can now help to improve the model and help guide the expansion needed. The new areas can now be absorbed without extensive reengineering of the data model or the data warehouse itself.

The GPT—LLM side

Any Generative Pre-Trained Model (GPT) uses a Large Language Model (LLM) and is trained to answer questions and make suggestions. The knowledge comes from all available data, which is absorbed from the internet and added to the LLMs. There is a lot of documentation on data and process modeling, which is, in theory, available to create data models and map any information into an organization. Unfortunately, millions of documents describe this process, and they are mostly written from an IT perspective (IT people have dominated this area from the start with articles, posts, and documentation on data and modeling). This means that "out of the box," the answers will be controversial and most likely not truly aligned with your organization.

Using the ELM approach as a basis for a data modeling GPT and limiting the documentation used in the LLM (making it a Smart Language Model or SML), will assist any organization in creating an understood and useful data model.

CHAPTER THREE

Running Workshops

Gathering the needed information within any domain/subject area/business function is key for success—just looking at what data is available in source systems won't do it. Running workshops with the business representatives is a great way of doing this. The workshops start communication and guide the process of working together. The whole purpose of this guided process is to have a documented overview of Core Business Concepts (CBCs) and their Natural Business Relations (NBRs). These CBCs and NBRs will form the basis of a logical data model recognized by the business. This logical data model is a direct blueprint for any of the ensemble modeling patterns, such as Data Vault, Anchor Modeling, and Focal.

We can identify three phases: Align, Refine, and Design[1] (which can be roughly translated to the technical terms conceptual model, logical model, and physical model).

- **Align**: Gather the business concepts from the business and learn to understand their concerns and language. In ELM, the CBC-List and CBC-Canvas are the prominent templates in this phase.

---

[1] The Align, Refine, and Design approach was created by Steve Hoberman. It is described in the *Data Modeling Master Class Training Manual 10th Edition* (https://technicspub.com/data-modeling-master-class/) and in the *Align > Refine > Design*® NoSQL modeling series (https://technicspub.com/the-align-refine-design-series/).

- **Refine**: This is to understand how the business sees the relationships between the identified business concepts and their cardinality/grain/direction. In ELM, the Event-Canvas and NBR-Form are the templates for this phase.

- **Design**: The actual plotting of the business concepts and how they relate on the board (physical whiteboard or digital board). It is important to model the relationships identified in the Refine phase. These relationships are not just lines between two objects since a relationship can exist between two or more business concepts.

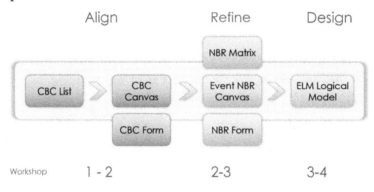

Figure 2: Artifacts overview.

In general, each phase will require one workshop, which will roughly take between one and three hours. This depends on the availability of the subject matter experts/business people and whether it is an online workshop or on-site at a physical location. Online workshops tend to be shorter, with a maximum of 1 ½ hours, due to less interaction between attendees. The workshop duration will also depend on the size of the domain/subject area/business function plus the attendees' experience with the ELM approach.

> *As a rule of thumb, plan a first workshop in an organization for 2 ½ hours in a physical location and 1 ½ hours for an online version. The actual time needed will guide you in the timing of the next workshops. Subsequent workshops tend to consume one hour for online workshops and two hours for on-site workshops (including break time).*

Although the ELM artifacts seem to have a strict order, this is not the case when running the actual workshops. The starting point for each domain/subject area/business function will be the first phase of the CBC-List—the listing of terms involved. The facilitator and the group can decide to use other artifacts, like the Event Canvas, if it helps with communication at that moment in time. Also, it is not a problem to return to artifacts if the discussion is on new terms, clearer definitions of terms, or for many other reasons. The process should feel natural to all. More experience in running and attending ELM workshops might lead to a different path. It is important, though, that, in the end, all ELM artifacts are documented.

The facilitator and scribe of these workshops will need an additional 8 to 12 hrs per workshop to process the input from the workshops into the artifacts and a baseline ELM model. The specific amount of time depends on the phase discussed in the workshop. The finalization of the CBC-Forms and NBR-Forms will be done after the workshop and is the business's responsibility. The data steward likely plays the main role in this process since it involves formalizing the business definitions and attributes (plus sample data on the NBR-Forms).

The first workshop sets the stage and starts with the first phase: Align. In the Align phase, the focus is on gathering the terms used in the organization or Core Business Concepts (CBCs) on the CBC-List. The second workshop will start with the overview/results of the Align phase done so far. It can continue into the Refine phase when there is agreement on all identified CBCs, their categorization, and their definitions. The same for the last workshop, where the design or modeling is the main activity. This can start with having another look and discussion on the Refine phase.

When moving forward to the next domain/subject area/business function, the first workshop will start with a blank CBC-List and CBC-Canvas.

This is to ensure that we capture all business concepts needed in the new domain/subject area/business function and to ensure that attendees feel free to bring their own input. After the first workshop (before workshop 2), there should be a consolidation of terms already mentioned earlier. The second workshop should start by comparing known business concepts with new business concepts. Special attention should be paid to those terms mentioned again to ensure the earlier definition remains the same.

> *Since communication (and embedding the CBCs in the model and the organization) is important, repeating the workshops for an already known domain/subject area/business function is a good idea. This repetition reconfirms that there is no change in terminology or relationships, especially when there is a big change in resources, such as involved SMEs and domain experts. This, of course, might lead to additional changes in the documentation and the model.*

The whole process appears in Figure 3 (as seen from the facilitator's view).

Invite for
workshop 1

Workshop 1

Homework

Workshop 2

Workshop 3

Present

Figure 3: Overview of workshops.

Invite the business people to the first workshop, the Align phase. Remember to not talk about a data modeling workshop but let it be known as a need for information on the domain/subject area/business function. A good trick is to include the remark, "donuts will be served with the coffee." In the ideal world, have the business sponsor send out the first invite. Otherwise, make sure to briefly introduce yourself and the assignment.

AVOID all references to technical terms. Don't say: "We need to create a data warehouse and reporting solution and would like your help to create the new data model." Or "We are here to replace the current data solution and need to hear from you about the issues in your reporting/dashboards." You don't want to focus on what is wrong or is missing from a current situation.

RATHER, let the invitees know you are curious about their work/organization. Say: "I am asked by … to help you get better and easier access to your information. For that, I would love some of your time to hear from you more about the domain/subject area/business function and discuss your information needs and that of your peers."

It is important to be well prepared. Be in the room long before any of the people arrive. Make sure you have the donuts/stroopwafels on the table, a clean whiteboard/flip chart, enough markers and Post-its, and blank templates printed out (laminated is great for re-usability). These are for extra note-taking. Ensure you have someone in the room to help you with note-taking and helping the facilitator (the scribe).

In case of a virtual online workshop, prepare a Miro board (or similar) and make sure it is accessible for all attendees, but don't share the link in the invite! The Canvasses must be ready to drag to the correct area on these online boards. Have the session running at least 10 minutes before the actual start of the workshop.

Start the first workshop with a small introduction round, even if people already seem to know each other. What is their function or area of expertise? Also, introduce yourself, your assignment, and the people helping you in the workshop. Again, avoid using technical terms and references. Tell attendees that you would rather have the group tell you what is going on than you asking the questions. The workshops are all about communication and conversation. If possible and allowed, you can record the session. Of course, always ask if people object, and make clear it is only to capture the business terms and jargon you might not be familiar with. The end result of this first workshop should be the capture and categorizing of the business terms.

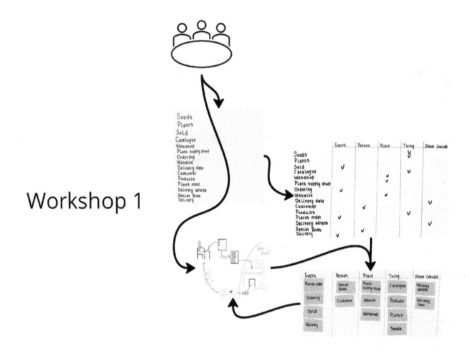

Figure 4: Workshop 1.

During the workshops, ensure everybody feels safe contributing to the discussion. All input is valuable. Also, invite people to the whiteboard to write down their ideas and visualize part of the process. Encourage discussions about terms and business functions within the group, so long as the discussions respect all opinions. All remarks and questions should be informative and not directive. Don't have laptops in the workshop, as there is rarely a need to look at the current information/dashboards during the workshops.

At the end of each workshop, thank the people for sharing their stories and make sure to have a final round for people to ask a last question or make a last remark. Also, inform people what they should do after workshop 1. The homework will consist of providing a short definition for all the terms mentioned and thinking about how these can be recognized and identified.

Start each following workshop by thanking the people for doing their "homework" and write down any remaining questions you received between workshops. Next, show the results of what has been done so far, show the canvasses/templates, and discuss if this is still correct. At any point in time, there can be an important new insight. Take the time to discuss this, especially if it was mentioned before and has already been discussed. If terms come back again, they are either ambiguous or not clear enough.

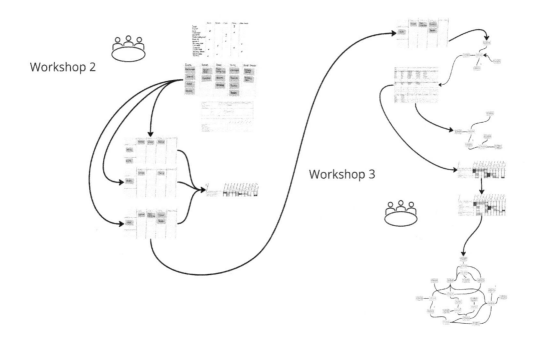

Figure 5: Workshops 2 and 3.

Workshops 2 and 3 will pick up on what was done in the prior workshops and start with discovering the relationships and the first start of a model.

The final stage is presenting the resulting ELM data model to the stakeholders. Since they were involved in the whole process, plus we keep using their own terminology, this should not feel like a technical story that is not close to their domain. The presentation of the result should confirm the model, but it might lead to additional questions and adjustments. That should not be seen as a failure, but proof that the communication between business and IT is succeeding.

Present

Figure 6: Present.

CHAPTER FOUR

Use of GPTs and LLMs for Data Modeling

The current landscape of GPTs and LLMs is changing rapidly, and the possibilities do not seem to have any boundaries. Also, in the field of data modeling, there are already a set of interesting opportunities and, without a doubt, more will become available in the future. In the summer of 2024, I made the first steps in developing a GPT capable of assisting in data modeling, the Genesee Academy modeling GPT. In the rapidly changing AI-landscape, I believe understanding the process of discovering and mapping a business toward a data model remains important. I also discovered that to train the GPT into what it needs to do, following the ELM approach steps seems logical. The ELM approach is designed to take small steps to keep everyone on board and make sure the result is in terms understood by the business, and this is also a perfect approach for AI.

With the assistance of the Genesee Academy modeling GPT, it is possible to have an extra assistant in finding the CBCs and their relationships. It is important to understand it will only provide a suggestion of the terms to use, including a short definition. The Genesee Academy modeling GPT will not replace actual input or discussion with the business people in workshops but rather must be seen as a valuable extra tool that can be used.

The input for the modeling GPT will be the business description of the domain/subject area/business function. It can be extended by a script of the recording of the first workshop and any available documentation. When writing this book, the modeling GPT can deliver the following ELM templates: CBC-List, including the categorization and a small definition. The Event-Canvas in written text, plus a suggestion for all other relationships. It will also assist you in determining what questions to ask in subsequent workshops. Without a doubt, there will be improvements and more precision in the modeling GPT over time.

The suggested use of this modeling GPT is to run an iteration in preparation for the first workshop, especially if the facilitator is unfamiliar with the organization or industry. Another option is to run the business case after the first workshop, including recording the first workshop and discussing the results in workshop 2. Of course, only if a recording is available and there is permission to use this. Also, including documentation as input seems promising and very valuable. Especially if there is a lot of documentation that is hard to grasp by merely reading and highlighting. The modeling GPT is truly an assistant for both the facilitator and the organizations to see, if possible, important CBCs and relationships that were missing and will be a valuable new asset in the ELM approach.

CHAPTER FIVE

The ELM Artifacts

There are six different artifacts, each with its own focus and goal. Using these artifacts will ensure you end up with a documented Ensemble Logical Model:

1. **CBC-List**: A listing of all named Core Business Concepts, categorized into "Event/Person/Place/Thing/Other."

2. **CBC-Canvas**: A canvas artifact to guide and visualize the process of discussing synonyms, hierarchies, levels, etc. Plus, discussing missing Core Business Concepts.

3. **CBC-Form**: A form for CBC disambiguation that provides a brief description/definition, including certain attribution, related events, subject areas, synonyms, etc.

4. **Event-Canvas**: Artifact that helps with the design and refinement of relationships. Also, this is an important document for data delivery teams.

5. **NBR-Matrix**: A listing of all named Natural Business Relations. This will hold all relations identified from the events and all other unique, specific NBRs recognized in the ELM process.

6. **NBR-Form**; A Form used to describe the relationship plus investigate the right grain, precision, and cardinality of the relation.

---

1. CBC-List

The CBC-List lists all the Core Business Concepts mentioned during the ELM workshop or interviews. In the ELM workshops and business interviews, representatives from the business will be asked about their business function, daily work and responsibilities, role, and activities (ask the 5, 6, or 7 W-questions). The named Core Business Concepts, basically all verbs and nouns mentioned in the ELM workshops and business interviews, are the Events, Persons, Places, and Things that are important to the business. In other words, they want and need to know more about these terms.

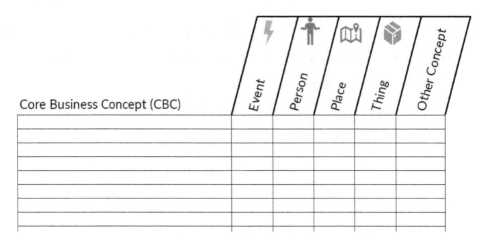

Figure 7: CBC-List.

The CBC-List will record all the verbs and nouns used by the business, as discussed in the workshops. All words will be listed, even if it seems like synonyms (Customer, Client, Kund) or groupings (Product, Coffee, Book).

This is important in this stage of the modeling process since we do not want to miss any of the words used by the business. It also reflects their own words and is thus recognized by the business.

Core Business Concept (CBC)	Event	Person	Place	Thing	Other Concept
Customer					
Sale					
Product					
Store					
Employee					
Kund					
Coffee					
Book					
Client					
Supplier					
Delivery					
Comment					

Figure 8: CBC-List example.

The next step on the CBC-List is to assign each listed CBC into its own category: Event, Person, Place, Thing, or Other. The sole purpose of this categorization is to help understand the business terms and understand if synonyms, hierarchies, or abstractions are mentioned. We can find these only within each category. That is, something categorized as a place can never be similar to something categorized as a person.

- **Event:** Most likely the verbs or nouns of a verb (like <u>Sale</u> is a noun related to the verb <u>Sell)</u>. This indicates something is happening or being done in the business function.

- **Person**: This could be any natural person or organization that is involved in the business function. This could be the originator or receiver, or the supporting or responsible role within the business function.

- **Place**: Any location, for instance, a physical building, property, or unit that is involved in the business function. It could also be a virtual location like a website.

- **Thing**: An object (often a physical object) that is involved in the business function. It could be an input, output, or something used by the business.

- **Other Concept**: Can be used if it is an important concept mentioned in the business interview, such as comment or Sale Line Item. These cannot be readily identified as any of the other categories, but they are important.

Core Business Concept (CBC)	Event	Person	Place	Thing	Other Concept
Customer		x			
Sale	x				
Product				x	
Store			x		
Employee		x			
Kund		x			
Coffee				x	
Book				x	
Client		x			
Supplier					x
Delivery	x				
Comment					x

Figure 9: CBC-List complete.

The goal of marking each Core Business Concept is to make sure we have a complete overview of the business we are looking into. The categorization will also help you to visualize and will be the input for the CBC-Canvas.

Use the CBC-List in every following workshop and business interview. Based on the situation, group of people, and organization, this could be in addition to the already used and completed CBC-List. However, start with a blank CBC-List when starting the first workshop for a new domain, subject area, or business function (see running the workshop).

Pay extra attention to all terms in the Other Concept category. When discussing these terms with the business, there is a chance that the mentioned term is not a true CBC. Since we don't discriminate on the terms, the business can mention a term that can be a Key Performance Indicator (KPI), derived term (like revenue, discount, etc.), context term (like address), relationship (like cast), or grouping (like product type). Using the CBC-Form will help discover whether it is a true CBC. If you can uniquely define the term, it has a unique identifier, and contains three to seven attributes, it will truly be a CBC.

2. CBC-Canvas

The CBC-Canvas is the ELM Artifact where we will group the CBCs from the CBC-List per category to investigate possible deduping or missing CBCs. This can be prepared by the facilitator of the ELM workshop or discussed in the ELM workshop.

Place the identified Core Business Concepts from the CBC-List in the corresponding column on the CBC-Canvas. This is especially helpful when there are many identified CBCs, and there is a need to look at possible synonyms or missing CBCs. This grouping per category will guide this process.

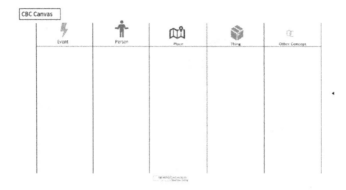

Figure 10: CBC-Canvas.

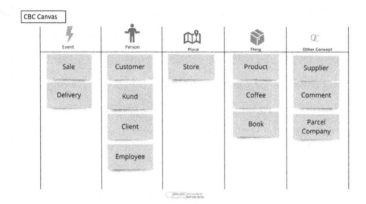

Figure 11: CBC-Canvas example.

In this example, the group in the workshop can decide that Customer, Kund, and Client are all synonyms of each other and decide to use the name Customer in the Logical model. Note that the terms Kund and Client will NOT be removed from the CBC-List. These will only refer to Customer.

In the same example, Product, Coffee, and Book are a hierarchy where Coffee and Book are at the lower level within the generic Product. From a Sales perspective, Product can be used, whereas from a Delivery perspective (and maybe future business functions to investigate), Coffee and Book are the important CBCs. This is another reason not to remove these from the CBC-List.

When using physical Post-its, it is a good practice to stick the Post-it notes on top of each other with the name to use on top. Figure 12 shows the hierarchy and the result of the discovery of the synonyms.

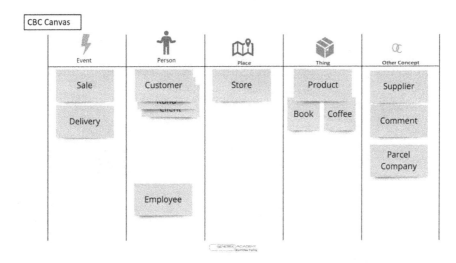

Figure 12: CBC-Canvas end.

3. CBC-Form

The CBC-Form is the ELM Artifact where we document all the CBCs, providing a brief description or definition, including certain attributions, related events, subject areas, synonyms, etc. Although most organizations have some kind of Business Glossary (complete or partial, up-to-date or outdated), it is not the idea to copy these into another format or use this as the starting point for the documentation. The CBC-Form is very helpful in the discussions to help determine if a CBC is really a CBC, can be seen as a synonym, or needs to be more specific. This form also helps a group better understand their own terminology and keep each member involved in the whole ELM process.

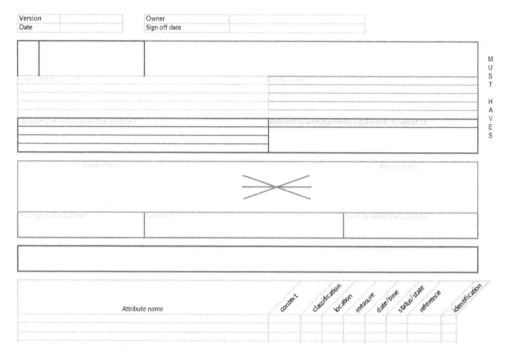

Figure 13: CBC-Form.

The following can be found on the CBC-Form:

- **CBC name**: The name of the Core Business Concept as mentioned by the business representatives. This should be a recognizable and identifiable name that the business understands.

- **CBC short definition**: A definition of the CBC which is just enough to understand the meaning of the CBC. We do not need a finite and exhausting definition since we are not trying to find a complete Master Data Management Definition.

- **Main context attributes**: The first couple of context attributes that come to mind when describing the CBC. In the process of agreeing upon whether a CBC is its own thing or a synonym, this is an important step in that discussion.

- **Subject Area**: Areas in the organization where the CBC is used and can be found.

- **Identifier:** How do we identify the CBC? It is not so much technical as well as in terminology. It could consist of multiple attributes that are substitutes or alternatives or that need to be combined to create a unique identifier.

- **Reference to workshop/model requirement**: It is good to note which workshop/document, etc., the CBC is named and defined.

- **Related CBCs**: Which CBCs can be related to the CBC? Think of CBC Store can be related to Region (as a CBC), Employee, Branch, etc.

- **Related events**: Which events can be related to the CBC. Thinking of CBC Store can be related to Sales, Delivery, etc.

- **Could be**: A Sub classification, lower (more specific) levels of CBC. Think of Book and Coffee as subcategories of Product. Often, it refers to hierarchies where the lower-level s within the hierarchy can be recognized as their own CBC.

- **Synonyms**: Alternative names/synonyms for the CBC which have the same meaning. In the ELM, it is recommended to use the more commonly known term as the CBC, and note the alternative names/synonyms. Of course, in the data distribution, these can be used to have a fit with the data consumer.

- **Higher-level concepts**: Indicates that the CBC is part of a grouping, e.g., Customer has Customer Class as a higher-level concept.

- **Context attribution**: Descriptive attributes, which are all the attributes and context describing the CBC. Classifying these attributes will be very useful when designing the Satellites (in Data Vault) or Descriptor tables (in Focal).

In general, the CBC-Form will be started in any ELM workshop or interview to clarify what a named CBC means and ensure everyone is on the same page. The CBC-Form will eventually be the complete documentation of any Core Business Concept.

During the ELM workshops, the documentation of a CBC can start in the CBC-Form to clarify what is meant and to decide about the disambiguation of a CBC.

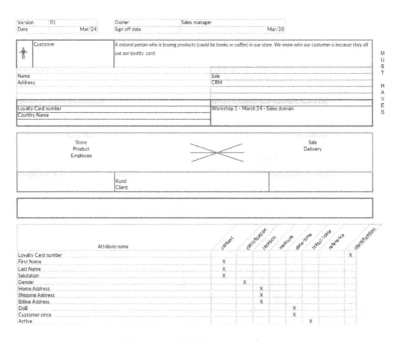

Figure 14: CBC-Form complete.

Parts 1 to 5 of the CBC-Form are must-haves for all identified CBCs to be modeled in the Ensemble Logical Model. Only if there is a clear name, definition (short), some context, an idea of the subject area, and the identifier of the CBC do we know what it is and how the business sees it.

The remainder of the CBC-Form can be filled in later. Of course, Business Glossaries and Master Data Management initiatives will help create a fully documented CBC-Form.

4. Event-Canvas

The Event-Canvas is an artifact that helps design and refine the relationships. Although it looks similar to the CBC-Canvas, the use and purpose are completely different. In the CBC-Canvas, we look for missing CBCs plus possible synonyms, deduping, and hierarchies. With the Event-Canvas, the focus is completely on <u>one</u> Event and all natural-related CBCs from a business perspective.

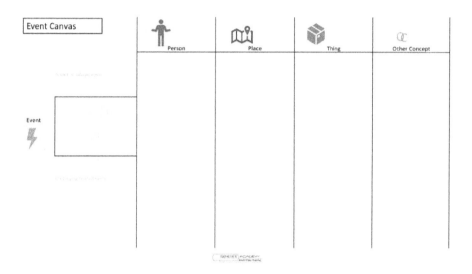

Figure 15: Event Canvas.

The idea behind the Event-Canvas is to give an overview of all involved CBCs per Event plus any adjusting Events that take place prior to or after the Event on the Canvas.

In this example, the focus is on a Sales event. Within the workshop, the conclusion is that Customer, Employee, Store, and Product are all involved whenever a Sale happens. For example, *"A Customer comes into the Store and buys one or more Products from the Employee."* This will be input for the next artifacts, the NBR-Matrix and NBR-Form, where we can check if one event might lead to multiple relations. This will occur whenever we find sparsity and redundancy in the relation or find out a relation is not unique.

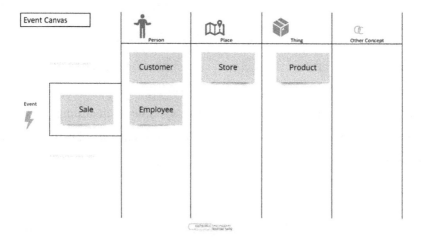

Figure 16: Event Canvas Sales example.

The Event-Canvas also has a place to identify closely related events, either because these can only occur when the other event happened or they happen simultaneously. See Figure 17, where Delivery is another event that can only occur when a Sale has happened. "*We only ship products we sold.*"

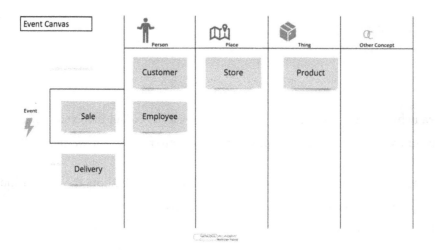

Figure 17: Event Canvas Sales example plus delivery.

Of course, the Delivery event can be captured in an Event-Canvas of its own with the involved CBCs for the Delivery event.

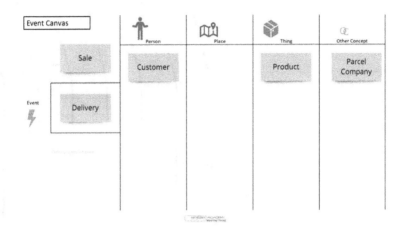

Figure 18: Event Canvas Delivery example.

The Event-Canvas will also guide your data consumption and is a perfect handover to the data delivery team to see which dimensions are related to the facts (usually coming out of events).

5. NBR-Matrix

The NBR-Matrix is a listing of all named Natural Business Relations. This will hold all relations identified from the events depicted on the Event-Canvas and all other unique, specific NBRs recognized in the ELM process. On the NBR-Matrix all involved CBCs will be checked for each Natural Business Relation they are related to. In other words, on each identified NBR, there is a checkmark for all identified CBCs needed to form that relation. Use two different shades of checkmark allows one to check if it is an involved CBC or the CBC is actually the originator of the NBR (which is true in the case of a CBC representing an event).

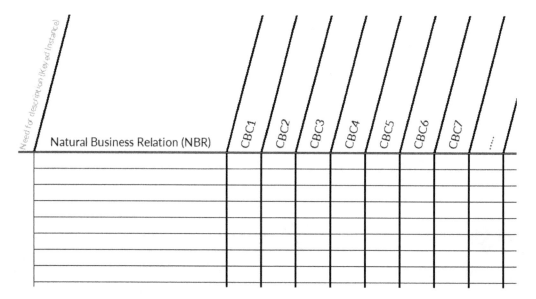

Figure 19: NBR-Matrix.

The NBR-Matrix is the artifact that captures the event-based relations, the unique and specific NBRs, and the involved CBCs. This is also the artifact where there will be some iteration and addition after discovering more on each of the initial NBRs. This discovery will be made when using the NBR-Form, the final ELM artifact, where we can discover example records for each NBR redundancy and uncover sparsity. In which redundancy will lead to header and detail relations and sparsity to additional unique, specific relations.

This is a combination of the two Event-Canvases from the example into one matrix. This gives an immediate overview of the two identified relations, each of which originated from its own event, Sales and Delivery. The next step is to discover if the identified NBRs are unique and specific, meaning there is no redundancy and no optional CBCs are involved. This can be discovered during the workshop or business interview or via the NBR-Form. This is similar to the interaction between CBC-List, CBC-Canvas, and CBC-Form, where more CBCs can be discovered or identified as synonyms or different levels (or hierarchies).

Need for description (Keyed Instance)	Natural Business Relation (NBR)	Sale	Customer	Store	Employee	Product	Delivery	Parcel company	....
	Sale Product to Customer	x	x	x	x	x			
	Delivery of Goods		x				x	x	

Figure 20: NBR-Matrix example iteration 1.

In this example, there is a difference between in-store sales (always an employee involved) and online sales (no employee involvement). On the NBR-Matrix, this would be as follows:

Need for description (Keyed Instance)	Natural Business Relation (NBR)	Sale	Customer	Store	Employee	Product	Delivery	Parcel company	....
	Sale Product to Customer	x	x	x	x	x			
	In Store Sale	x	x	x	x	x			
	Online Sale	x	x	x		x			
	Delivery of Goods		x				x	x	

Figure 21: NBR-Matrix example iteration 2.

The indent of the in-store and online sale NBR indicates that these are both a more precise and detailed level of NBR. There can be multiple indents to indicate a more detailed NBR can be found.

We might discover the detection of header and detail information in a future iteration. In this example, there would be a repetition of sale, customer, employee, and store (or sale, customer, and store) for each product on a sale. The next step to prevent this redundant information is to create a header and detailed relation around sale.

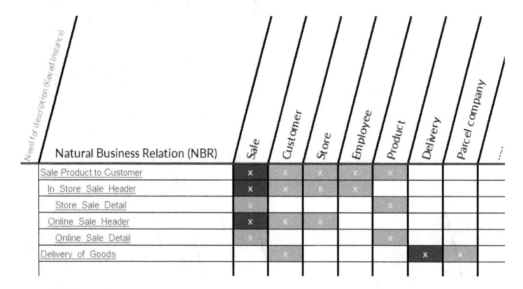

Natural Business Relation (NBR)	Sale	Customer	Store	Employee	Product	Delivery	Parcel company	...
Sale Product to Customer	x	x	x	x	x			
In Store Sale Header	x	x	x	x				
Store Sale Detail	x				x			
Online Sale Header	x	x	x					
Online Sale Detail	x				x			
Delivery of Goods			x			x	x	

Figure 22: NBR-Matrix example iteration 3.

Since, in this example, it is logical that there is a need to capture the amount and pricing of each product on sale, and line item is not yet identified as its own CBC, there is a need to have that identified as well.

This will lead the Ensemble Logical Model to a Relationship Describing Hub, which is also the CBC "owning" the relationship. Hence, the dark green color. The details on each of these NBRs can be found on the NBR-Form.

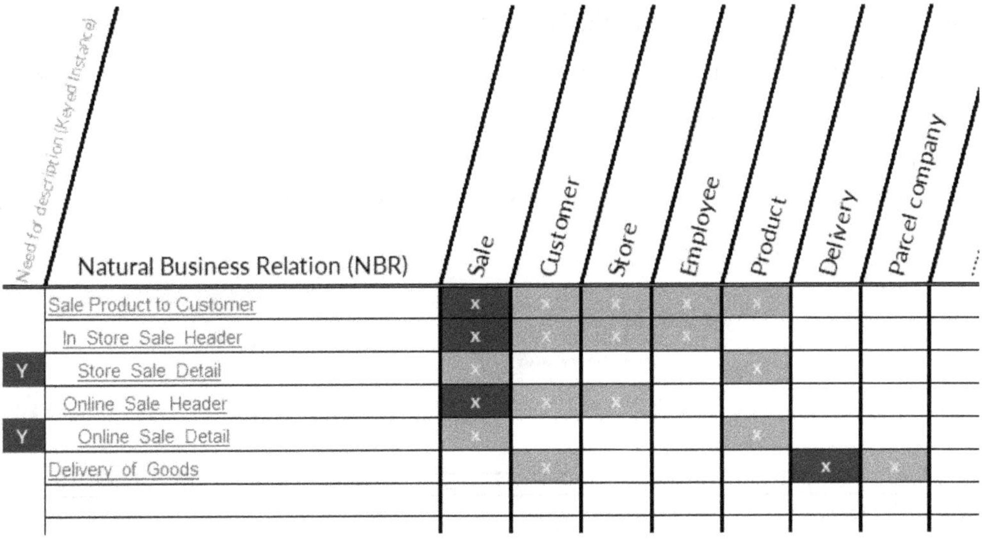

Natural Business Relation (NBR)	Sale	Customer	Store	Employee	Product	Delivery	Parcel company	...
Sale Product to Customer	x	x	x	x	x			
In_Store_Sale_Header	x	x	x					
Store_Sale_Detail	x				x			
Online_Sale_Header	x	x	x					
Online_Sale_Detail	x				x			
Delivery_of_Goods		x				x	x	

Figure 23: NBR-Matrix Final.

6. NBR-Form

The NBR-Form is used to describe the relationship plus investigate the grain, precision, and cardinality of the relation. The NBR-Matrix, which is a summary or aggregation of all identified relations on the Event-Canvas, is the starting point to further describe the involved relations and discover additional relationships. For each of the identified NBRs, there will be a filled-in NBR-Form.

The following can be found on the NBR-Form:

- **Reference to workshop/model requirement**: It is good to keep note of which workshop/document, etc., the NBR is named and defined.

- **NBR-Name**: The name of the Natural Business Relation as mentioned by the business representatives. This should be a recognizable and identifiable name that the business understands.

- **NBR short definition**: A definition of the NBR that is just enough to understand its meaning.

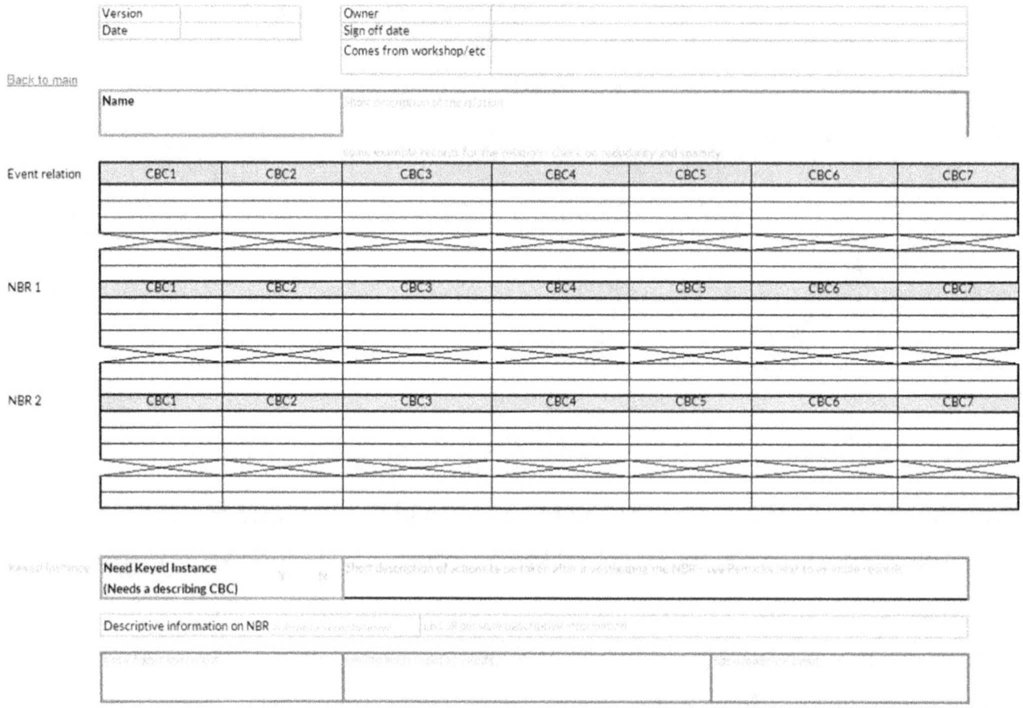

Figure 24: NBR-Form.

- **Example records**: There will be some example records for each of the involved CBCs in the NBR. In general, use Hans and Remco instead of 778865 and 887757 for customer. The example records need to be understood. Important, do not use measures or generic attribution like amount (235), price (€10,95), or score (B+), since these are purely descriptive information and do not relate to an identifier.

- **Need Keyed Instance**: A tick box to quickly identify if there is a need for a Keyed instance in this relationship. In other words, we need to describe or relate to it.

- **A short description of actions to be taken after investigating the NBR**: When filling in the example records, there is a need for header and detail relations.

- **Involved CBCs**: Which CBCs are identified as having a part in this NBR.

- **Descriptive information on NBR**: What kind of information is needed to describe the relation? This will form the start of attribution of the keyed instance hub.

- **Has a higher-level event**. Indicates that the NBR has a more aggregated relation associated with it. In most cases, this indicates that the Event within a CBC has a header relationship as well as a detail relationship.

- **Simultaneous events**. If there is an associated event that occurs or could occur with the described NBR.

- **Has a lower-level event**. Indicates that the NBR has a more detailed relation associated with it. In most cases, this indicates that the Event within a CBC has a detailed relationship as well as a header relationship.

This example is a direct translation of the NBR related to the sale event, which can be found in the NBR-Matrix. With the writing of the definition plus the example records, it is clear that there is redundancy and sparsity to be found in this original NBR. In the end, this will lead to a header and detailed link for both in-store and online sales, as shown in Figure 25. At the end of the process, for all identified and discovered NBRs, an NBR-Form should be completed, as shown in Figure 26.

Version	4	Owner	
Date	01/05	Sign off date	
		Comes from workshop/etc	Workshop 3 – May 1 - Sales domain

Back to main

Sale Product to Customer	The actual selling of products to our customers in our physical store or online store supported by our employees....

Event relation
In Store Sale

Sale	Customer	Store	Employee	Product	CBC6	CBC7
501	Remco	Utrecht	Hans	Moby Dick		
501	Remco	Utrecht	Hans	Newspaper		
501	Remco	Utrecht	Hans	Coffee		
501	Remco	Utrecht	Hans	Hitchhikers guide		
2345	Carl	www.ourshop.com		Modeling the Agile		
2345	Carl	www.ourshop.com		Post-Its		
etc.						

Online Sale

NBR 1

CBC1	CBC2	CBC3	CBC4	CBC5	CBC6	CBC7

NBR 2

CBC1	CBC2	CBC3	CBC4	CBC5	CBC6	CBC7

Need Keyed Instance (Needs a describing CBC)	Y N	
Descriptive information on NBR		

Figure 25: NBR-Form example iteration 1.

Version	4	Owner	Sales manager	
Date	01/05	Sign off date		01/05
		Comes from workshop/etc	Workshop 3 – May 1 - Sales domain	

Back to main

Sale Product to Customer In Store	The actual selling of products to our customers in our physical store supported by our employees.

Event relation

Sale	Customer	Store	Employee	Product	CBC6	CBC7
501	Remco	Utrecht	Hans	Moby Dick		
501	Remco	Utrecht	Hans	Newspaper		
501	Remco	Utrecht	Hans	Coffee		
501	Remco	Utrecht	Hans	Hitchhikers guide		
etc.						

NBR 1

Sale	Customer	Store	Employee	CBC5	CBC6	CBC7
501	Remco	Utrecht	Hans			
etc.						

NBR 2

Sale	Product	CBC 3	CBC4	CBC5	CBC6	CBC7
501	Moby Dick					
501	Newspaper					
501	Coffee					
501	Hitchhikers guide					
etc.						

Need Keyed Instance (Needs a describing CBC)	Y N	Create the Relationship Describing Hub / Keyed Instance to describe products on a Sale. Need to concatenate Sale number with the actual Line Item
Descriptive information on NBR		Amount, Price, Discount, VAT

Figure 26: NBR-Form example final.

CHAPTER SIX

The Ontology

The ontology is a guide to categorizing and understanding CBCs, NBRs, and Context. The starting point in the ontology is the business term. See the QR code to Shared Drive:

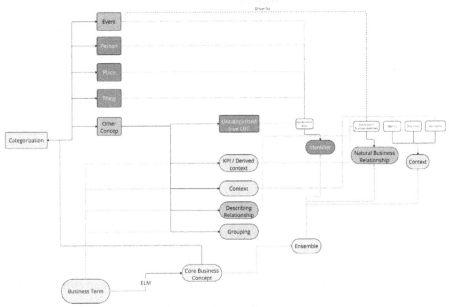

Figure 27: Ontology.

From the named Business Term, there is a breakdown into CBCs, KPIs, Derived Metrics, Context, Grouping Terms, and Descriptions of Relationships. Those business terms recognized as core business concepts will form the ensembles in the logical model, which contains the identifier, all relationships, and context.

- **Business Term**: All the terms an organization uses to describe and run their business. These terms will be verbs and nouns used in any business case.

- **Ensemble**: Ensembles contain one instance identifier (some form of key to uniquely identify an instance throughout the enterprise), the relationships that it drives (relationships between it and other Ensembles), and the descriptive context that describes (and depends) on that instance/key. There is a strict 1 to 1 relationship between CBC and Ensemble. An ensemble represents an event, person, thing, place, or other concept in a Data Vault model. The ensemble is the general equivalent of the entity in a traditional relational model (such as third normal form or 3NF). It is also similar to the concept in conceptual modeling and can be generally recognized as a dimension in dimensional modeling.

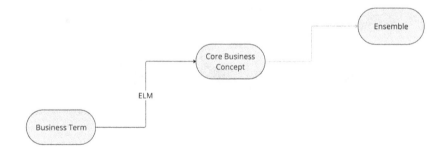

Figure 28: Ontology starting point.

- **Core Business Concept**: These are the fundamental Event, Person, Thing, Place, and Other Concept names used in the day-to-day operations in running the business or organization. They are the business terms spoken, the subjects of emails, the nouns in the questions asked, and the most commonly referenced in the organization. These are the business terms that can be uniquely identified and defined. These are distinguished from other business terms that describe metrics, context, and KPIs (might be defined but do not hold unique identifiers to describe it), or groupings and hierarchies (might hold unique identifiers but are hard to define uniquely). A CBC is specifically not a technical construct, nor is it a generalized or abstracted concept.

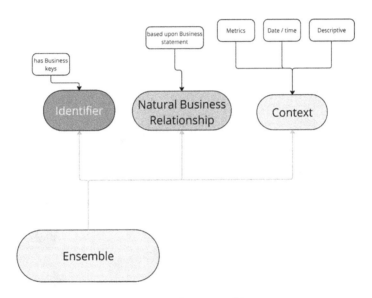

Figure 29: Ontology Ensemble.

- **Identifier**: The unique identification of an Ensemble from a business perspective. Since business terms are not bound to a domain, the identifier can consist of multiple parts. There is no direct relation to any source system, as these are enterprise concepts. However, it can be that part of the identifier from the business is directly associated with a certain business area or source system.

- **Natural Business Relationship**: This describes how the identified CBCs are related to each other based on how the organization understands them. All NBRs should be unique and specific. There will be multiple relations if the organization can interpret several relationships between the same CBCs. This is specifically not a technical construct, nor is it a generalized or abstracted concept.

- **Context**: The Data Vault Ensemble context is modeled in Satellites. There can be several satellites describing a single instance of a Hub. These satellites are designed by considering the type of data, the rate of change, and, in some cases, the source system (if leapfrogging or sparsity is observed as a problem). Satellites are all pre-built for historical tracking. Satellites are the only construct capable of tracking history as they are the only ones to have a two-part key (including the Inscription Timestamp/Load Date Time field).

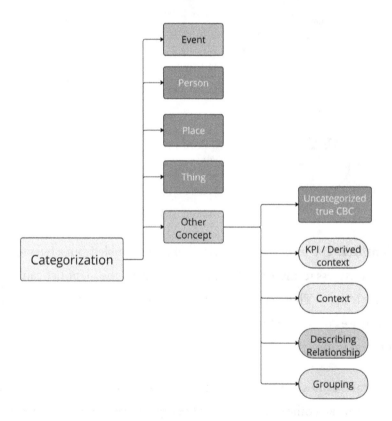

Figure 30: Ontology Categorization.

- **Categorization**: Distinction into different categories. The sole purpose of this categorization is to help understand the business terms and, optionally, their synonyms, hierarchies, or abstractions. These can only be found within each category. Something that is categorized as a place can never be similar to something categorized as a person.

- **Event**: Most likely the verbs or nouns of a verb (like Sale is a noun related to the verb Sell). This indicates something is happening or being done in the business function.

- **Person**: This could be any natural person or organization involved in the business function. This could be the originator, receiver, or the supporting responsible role within the business function.

- **Place**: Any location. For instance, a physical building, property, or unit involved in the business function. It could also be a virtual location like a website.

- **Thing**: An object (often a physical object but not limited to physical objects only) that is involved in the business function. It could be the input or output used in the business.

- **Other Concept**: This can be used if an important concept is mentioned in the business interview, e.g., a comment or Sale Line Item. These cannot be readily identified as any of the other categories, but they are important.

- **Grouping**: This can become a Natural Business Relationship, its own true Core Business Concept, or an attribute used for grouping in reports/dashboards.

CHAPTER SEVEN

The ELM Approach Applied to Willibald

This chapter will describe how the ELM approach and the artifacts will guide you toward an Ensemble Logical Data Model using the publicly available "Willibald" case as provided by the German-speaking Data Vault User Group—DDVUG (see www.dwa-compare.info). The case originated as a way to compare different Data Vault automation tools and, as such, was presented at the TDWI conference in Munich in 2023. I will use the same case to mimic the whole process and map the business into a logical data model. You can see this as an example of applying the ELM approach and using its artifacts within your organization.

Introducing Willibald

The company Willibald is a traditional business that trades seeds and plants via the internet. In the past, the company sold exclusively via a catalog. The catalog was quickly terminated in 2000, a full four years after the web shop was opened. Willibald was the first plant supply shop on the internet and is still proud of it today.

Ordering is a very simple process. The customer selects his products and places his order. They can specify a delivery address for each order item. When ordering via the website, one can enter a desired delivery date, and this is currently met 90% of the time.

Delivery is then made on the desired date if possible. Since shipping plants also include shrubs and smaller trees, Willibald uses several delivery services.

The seeds and plants are listed in a product catalog. The product catalog is arranged hierarchically according to different categories.

The VereinsPartner is the backbone of Willibald's marketing. Since its foundation in 1926, the Willibald seed and plant shop has offered special conditions and discounts for allotment and horticultural associations (these being the VereinsPartner). For each association, there is a contact person among the customers. Each customer can register for their association and thus receive the association benefits. The senior boss of Willibald is convinced that this concept has brought the Willibald company through all crises.

The Willibald seed and plant trade goes on a roadshow twice a year. The allotment and horticultural associations are visited during this roadshow with a truck full of seeds and plants. It will organize a small festivity and sell diligently. 2% of the turnover from this truck is donated directly to the association. For Willibald, this is a very good opportunity to get the seasonal goods to the customer before they expire. Since the beginning of the roadshow, no seasonal goods have had to be composted.

The data from the roadshow comes from the cash register system. Each turnover is assigned to a club partner. The customer can enter his customer number. Unfortunately, only about 20% of the customers do this. Therefore, these turnovers cannot all be assigned to one customer.

My goal in this chapter is to give a practical insight into the templates' use and the steps to move toward a Logical Data Model that aligns with the organization. In the Willibald case, I will discuss some of the issues you can face during the whole process and, of course, what you can do to either prevent this from happening or encounter the hiccups when they occur. I am very grateful to Michael Müller for playing the role of the business counterpart in this process.

All documentation and artifacts can be found here:

After the initial contact with the senior boss of Willibald, we received permission to start with the ordering and sales process of Willibald. This was chosen because Willibald was having difficulty getting the correct information for reporting and having difficulty knowing how well they performed. So, we sent out the invites to the stakeholders involved in Willibald for this particular part of the organization.

Workshop 1: Align—phase CBC

As with any project, the Willibald case starts with understanding the business and capturing its jargon. That is, the actual wording used within the organization. The best way to discover these is to start with a workshop with all the business stakeholders in one room with a big whiteboard, markers, and lots of Post-its. In my invitation to the Willibald team, I invited them to introduce me to Willibald. What is it that they do? What is the history? How do they see themselves as an organization? What are the processes they are involved with or concerned about?

The reason for this first workshop and the questions is to get me aligned with their organization. During the workshop, I captured all the verbs and nouns mentioned while they told me about Willibald and how they run their business. And although I had the questions ready to be fired, the people in the workshop were basically telling the story in their own words. As a facilitator, I did not need to do much direct questioning. They were also filling in the gaps in each other's story, although the boss had the most to say.

If you notice in a workshop that people are afraid of telling their part of the story, it might be good to request that the dominant person keep silent or even stop attending the running workshop during a break. You need a safe environment during the workshop where all the people are heard and free to speak. In the Willibald case, I needed to address the senior boss to tune down his input and leave the workshop for some time (he suddenly had an urgent call ☺)

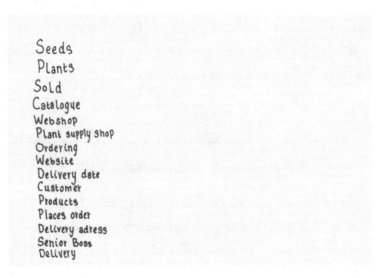

Figure 31: Willibald Whiteboard business terms.

With the words written down on a list, after a short break, we continued the workshop. With a focus on the sales, ordering, and delivery process, all terms are discussed again.

Although the delivery process was not mentioned in the original assignment, it became obvious that some of the pain points had to do with the delivery process. A lot of discussion was about order and delivery dates to calculate the delivery stats. The decision in the workshop was to include the delivery process as well.

This discussion is just to see if we missed any of the terms mentioned that are not in focus for the first iteration. During this part, I also made a quick drawing on the whiteboard to visualize their business and the process they are explaining to me. I often make these drawings to see if we are complete and missing important terms. In the Willibald case, we soon found that the actual packaging and warehouse part is part of the order, but delivery was excluded. There was too little insight into that part of the process and no interest in calculating revenue, turnover, and delivery accuracy.

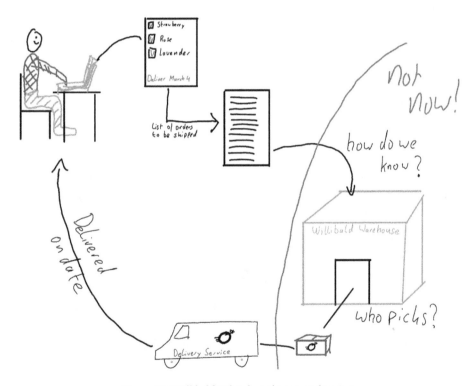

Figure 32: Willibald Whiteboard process drawing.

The next step in the same workshop is to categorize each CBC as an Event, Person, Place, Thing, or Other Concept. I emphasize this as an important step. We would see again if we missed something naming all the business terms and check if everyone in the workshop has the same idea with a term and if there are synonyms and hierarchies we need to consider.

	Event	Person	Place	Thing	Other Concept
Seeds				✓	
Plants				✓	
Sold	✓				
Catalogue				✓	
Webshop			✓		
Plant supply shop			✓		
Ordering	✓				
Website			✓		
Delivery date					✓
Customer		✓			
Products				✓	
Places order	✓				
Delivery adress					✓
Senior Boss		✓			
Delivery	✓				

Figure 33: Willibald Whiteboard CBC List.

A synonym can only occur if both terms belong to the same category. I never heard that a Person and a Place were seen as the same thing.

Sometimes, it is hard to categorize a CBC. This can happen if the term is ambiguous. For example, with "Order," people can define an order as the Event, as in 'a customer orders a coffee' or as a Thing, as in 'all that needs to be made was written on the order.' If that is the case, the terms need to be made clearer and more precise. "Ordering" for the Event and "Order" for the Thing. Or "Bed" for a Place (in a hospital, from a healthcare perspective) and "Physical Bed" as a Thing (the actual bed you can lie in for the maintenance department of a hospital).

In this step, we also discuss the level of detail we need to capture. In this case, we discussed whether it was important to capture seeds, shrubbery, plants, and trees or just call it product for now. The terms Website and Webshop were also discussed and identified as synonyms. This made Webshop the prevalent term to use.

Another point of attention is everything that is categorized in the Other Concept category. Since this category captures all terms not identified as Event, Person, Place, or Thing, we need to check if these terms are really CBCs or if they might be terms used for metrics or calculations, or for representing relationships/grouping or an identifier. Good examples in the Willibald case are "Turnover" and "Associations Benefit," which don't mean anything or have a clear definition or a true identifier. After some discussions, these were noted as metrics. Another example was "Customer number," which was mentioned to be hugely important, yet it is the identifier of a "Customer" and not a CBC on its own.

To guide this step, we created Post-its of all terms and put them in all columns marked as Event, Person, Place, Thing, and Other Concept. An extra benefit is that this really makes the workshop active for the attendees, inviting them to stand up and put the Post-its on the board themselves. At the end of the workshop, we had a complete list of all the CBCs mentioned and noted which were important for the first iteration. I worked out my notes and all that was captured on the whiteboard. See Figure 34.

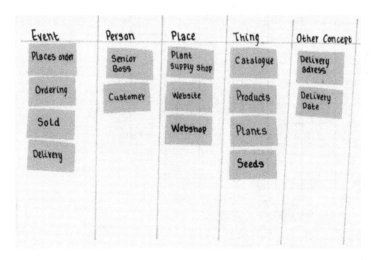

Figure 34: Willibald Whiteboard CBC Canvas.

With this input, I created the CBC-List, which contained the terms we wrote on the whiteboard added to the CBC-List template. I also created the CBC-Canvas based on the picture of the Post-its on the whiteboard organized per category. Finally, I created a CBC-Form for almost each of the terms on the CBC-List, synonyms with references to the term discussed as the prominent one to use, as well as for the grouping. In the Willibald example, seeds, plants, trees and shrubs were mentioned on the CBC-List but would reference the CBC-Form for Product. The sheet with the CBC-List and the CBC-Forms were sent to the Willibald team to complete. I asked the team to write down the definitions for each term and provide the important context or all they can think of in the corresponding CBC-Form. This homework was to be completed before the next workshop. I also added a couple of questions that needed to be clarified to make sure I am Aligned with Willibald. One of the questions that needed an answer was about using the term 'senior boss' without mentioning other types of employees or just employees.

CBC List	Event	Person	Place	Thing	Other Concept	Context	
Seeds						X	A type of product
Plants						X	A type of product
Sale	X						
Catalogue							Old name - is now webshop
Webshop			X				Website is a synonym
Plant supply shop						X	Chamber of Commerce Indication No SOURCE - Out of Scope now
Ordering	X						
Delivery date						X	Context on Customer and/or on Delivery/Shipping
Customer		X					
Product				X			"seeds, plants, trees, shrubs" are all products (which can be seasonal or not -> context)
Delivery address						X	Context on Customer and/or on Delivery/Shipping
Order item					X		
Delivery	X						Delivery & Shipping synonyms
Shipping	X						Delivery synonyms
Shrubs						X	A type of product
Trees						X	A type of product
Delivery services					X		
Vereinspartner		X					
Conditions						X	Context on Sale and Ordering
Discounts						X	Context on Sale and Ordering
Contact person						X	Context on Vereinspartner
Receive							The result of the delivery - not in scope
Associations benefits						X	Context on Sale and Ordering plus on Vereinspartner

> ··· CBC-List after 1st feedback Sale Webshop Ordering Delivery Customer Vereinspartner Senior boss Road show Product ··· + ︙ ◂

Figure 35: Willibald CBC List template.

Version	1
Date	01/07

Owner	Senior Boss	
Sign off date		07/07
Comes from workshop/etc	Workshop at Willibald Office with Management team d.d. 30/6	

⚡	Sale	The Sale of a product - can be plants, shrubs, seed, trees, etc. - to customers. The sale is only during roadshows. Based upon the totals of Sales during Roadshows Willibald will donate part of the revenue to the "vereinspartner"

Sale date (Kaufdatum) Price (Preis) Amount (Menge)	BestellungID

Customer Product Roadshow		.. ..

	Sell	

Name	describe	classify	locate	measure	date/time	status/state	reference	identity
Sale date (Kaufdatum)					x			
Price (Preis)				x				
Amount (Menge)				x				
Credit Card (Kreditkarte)	x							
Valid to (Gueltigbis)					x			
Credit Card Company (KKFirma)							x	
Sales ID (BestellungID)								x

Figure 36: Willibald CBC Form template.

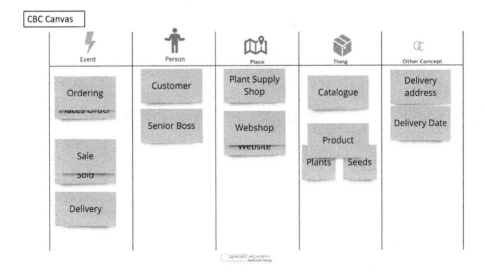

Figure 37: Willibald CBC Canvas.

Workshop 2 Refine—phase NBR

The second workshop started with another look at all the named CBCs to discover if we missed some. In other words, are we still Aligned with the business? We also discussed the mentioned "senior boss" again. Although we might need to have employees or the different types of employees as a CBC in the model, we decided to disregard them for now.

So, we continued with the completed CBC-List to Refine the CBCs and their definitions where needed. As a next step, it was time to discover what is related to what, or, in other words, find the relationships. The approach here is to take one event and discuss what the CBCs are and which are directly related to that event. For example, for a Sale, the product that sold is relevant, but the manufacturer or supplier of that product is not relevant.

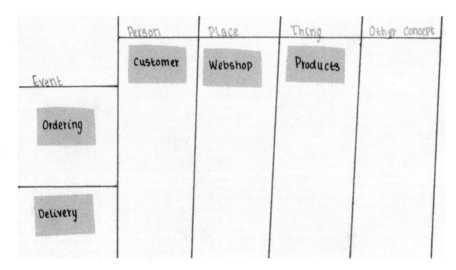

Figure 38: Willibald Whiteboard Event Canvas.

At this moment in the workshop, there is no notion of any of the source systems and it should not even feel like data modeling in a technical way. I avoid using terms like conceptual or logical data modeling, crow's foot notation, cardinality, etc., to avoid any confusion with the business people in the workshop and keep them on board.

As soon as we discover all the CBCs that are related to that one event, it is time for the next step. I start asking questions about the event. Tell me more about this event. Can an individual order multiple products in one order? Let's see some records to see what is known.

This is when I put Post-its on the board and start drawing the lines between them. If more things are directly related to each other (e.g., Order, Customer, web shop), I will let the lines come together in a "relationship" post-it. Adding a clear functional name or short functional description (e.g., Customer places order in a webshop) can be helpful in this stage. When digitalizing in the model, functional names are necessary for clear business understanding. This can be a short, functional sentence.

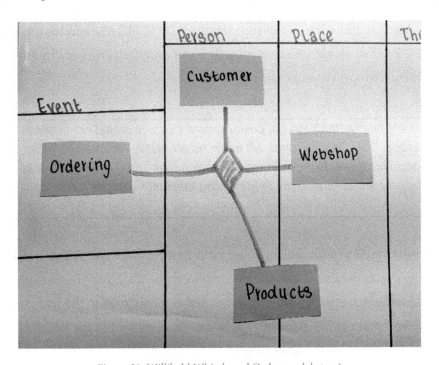

Figure 39: Willibald Whiteboard Order model step 1.

If we are happy with one event, I take a picture, clear the board, and start with the next event. Working on a clear board per event keeps the modeling simple, to the point, and less complex. At the end of the workshop, we are Aligned with the business and have Refined to the actual process.

If all events are done and we refine the relationship, we will also have an idea of what the output result needs to be and which facts against which dimensions need to be delivered to create the desired reports/dashboards. Although the focus is not on output nor creating a data warehouse, what we do in the workshops will lead toward an Aligned and Refined set of business terms with relationships. And since we are discussing this with the business, they will tell us what they need to know about a business term. In the Willibald case, it was all about the difference between the order and delivery dates.

Of course, any leftover terms that were not mentioned in any of the events need to be discussed. Are they related to any of the identified CBCs, like Manufacturer is related to Product and Product alone? Or are they really part of the focus we have in this phase? If not, then these terms will be out of scope as well.

> *At any point in the process, business terms can be added or set out of scope. Out-of-scope terms will never be physically removed from the lists. This prevents those terms from being mentioned again, including the previous discussions. I'm not saying that there can't be a change of priority.*

After this workshop, the notes will be added to the Event-canvas and NBR-Form, including some example records. This is also the moment to create the NBR-Matrix (the collection of all discovered relationships), which can be used as a handover to the team that creates the output layer and reports. As with all artifacts, these are sent to the Willibald team for verification. Since none of the artifacts used so far are different from what was written on the whiteboards or feel technical, the experience is that it is not a problem for the business team to understand these.

In our last workshop, I showed the digital design or ELM model to finalize as a first piece of work. I worked on Miro in the last workshop since it was a remote session. I use Post-its with the functional names as their business terms on the virtual whiteboard. The Post-its represent a relationship and will have a full description to represent that relationship in their wording. To stay close to what was done earlier, I only model per event. In other words, I write down all the terms on Post-its that belong to a certain event and place these on the whiteboard, draw the lines, and explain what I am doing and how this reflects what they told me.

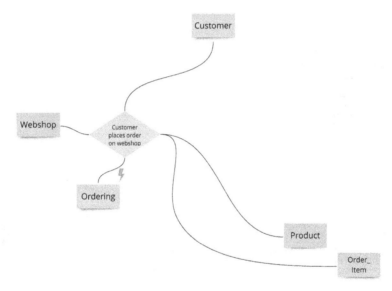

Figure 40: Willibald Whiteboard Order model step 1.

The model becomes clear when using different colored Post-its: blue for business terms/CBCs and green for relationships.

Adding a flash on the Post-it representing the event or using a slightly different color blue helps in understanding the visual representation.

Cardinality is captured through wording on the Post-it representing the relationship. In the Willibald case, we had "An order has one known Customer via a website" and "Every order can have more than one product." To make this clear we created some example records to see if we modeled on the correct grain.

Name						
Delivery		The Delivery of Products to Customer. Each delivery of a product is seen as its own unique delivery				

Delivery	Customer	Delivery Service	Order Item	Product	CBC6	CBC7
398 || 994	Bettina	Henne und Alter OHG	994	Knollensellerie		
398 || 995	Bettina	Henne und Alter OHG	995	Spinat		
398 || 996	Bettina	Kauer und Wisniewski Gmbl	996	Wildtomate		
678 || 1694	Elgine	Benja OHG	1694	Aubergine		
678 || 1695	Elgine	Benja OHG	1695	Buschbohne		
678 || 1696	Elgine	Benja OHG	1696	Kürbis		
CBC1	CBC2	CBC3	CBC4	CBC5	CBC6	CBC7
CBC1	CBC2	CBC3	CBC4	CBC5	CBC6	CBC7

Figure 41: Willibald NBR Form example records.

From these example records, we can clearly see a repetition of 'Ordering,' 'Customer,' and 'Webshop' for all the different products in a particular order on the Event relation. That is why we split this one relationship into two different relationships. This is, of course, a small change in the model, thanks to the Post-its on the whiteboard.

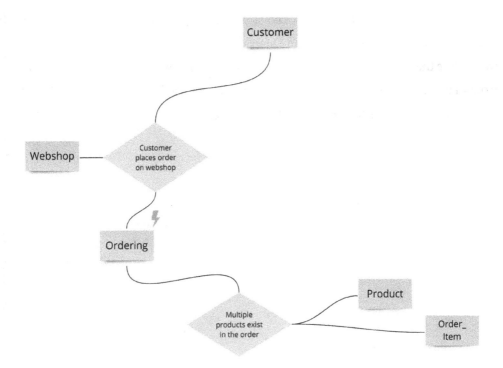

Figure 42: Willibald Whiteboard Order model refined.

Workshop 3 Design

The last step in the Design phase is to add any context we want to capture using yellow Post-its. As soon as we find out there is a need to describe a relationship, such as "How many products are there within an order?", we will add an extra blue Post-it. My explanation during this part of the workshop is that if we need to describe something that is apparently important for the business, we probably missed it before or didn't have a business term ready to use. In the case of the "amount of each product in an order," Willibald already mentioned Order Item, which is the technical name for "Product in an Order." In the design, I changed the name to the more business term "Product in an Order," with Order Item between brackets to have both represented.

When all is discussed and refined, I take a picture of the board for documentation. The next step is to clean the whiteboard and start with the next event. For example, the delivery event. Note that the delivery is related to the 'Order Item,' which basically means the actual Product within a certain Order. Since the business was used to 'Order Item' in Willibald, I didn't change the name to a more functional name.

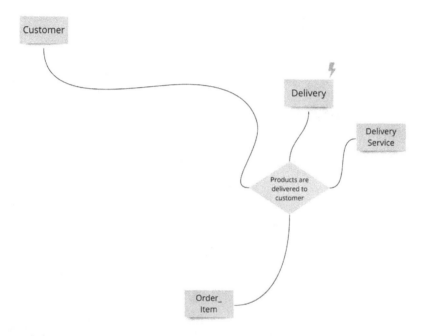

Figure 43: Willibald Whiteboard Delivery model.

During a break after all the events, I would use the photos to create one big model to show all that has been done. This one will also include all existing relationships without a direct known event. Using different colors for the lines can be very helpful in following each discussed event in the whole model. All the remarks made during the final walkthrough, like attention points for the next phase, are written on the side. Using different colors or numbering will align this to the events it reflects (if applicable).

At the end of the final workshop, we have the Design or ELM model, which can be translated one-to-one to a physical Data Vault model (or any ELM patterns like Focal or

Anchor). At the same time, we provided the reporting team with documentation on what they can expect and which data marts need to be created. Most importantly, it is easier to discuss their dashboarding and information needs with the business people since they speak the same language and use the same terms. It will also be easier to understand what is possible and not possible to include in the dashboards and reports, since these are directly related to their process, which they just walked through and discussed.

> Other modeling patterns like 3NF and dimensional modeling will also benefit from this approach and can use the same steps. Only the last design and modeling phase, especially the translation to a physical design, will be different using #NF or dimensional modeling.

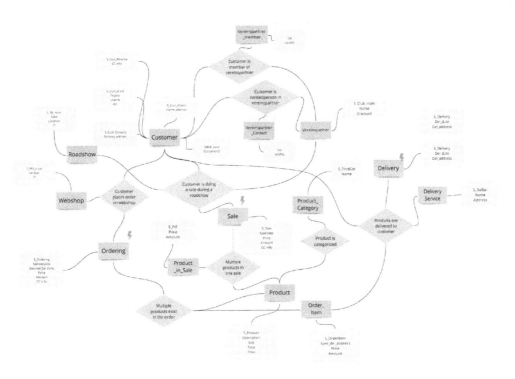

Figure 44: Visual 48 Willibald Whiteboard complete model.

CHAPTER EIGHT

The Templates for the Six Artifacts

You can also download these via www.ELMStandards.com.

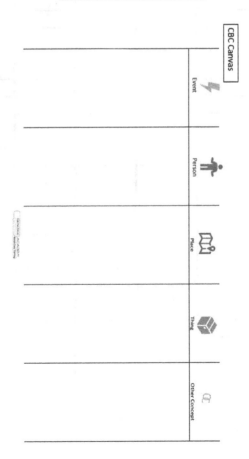

CBC List	Event	Person	Place	Thing	Other Concept

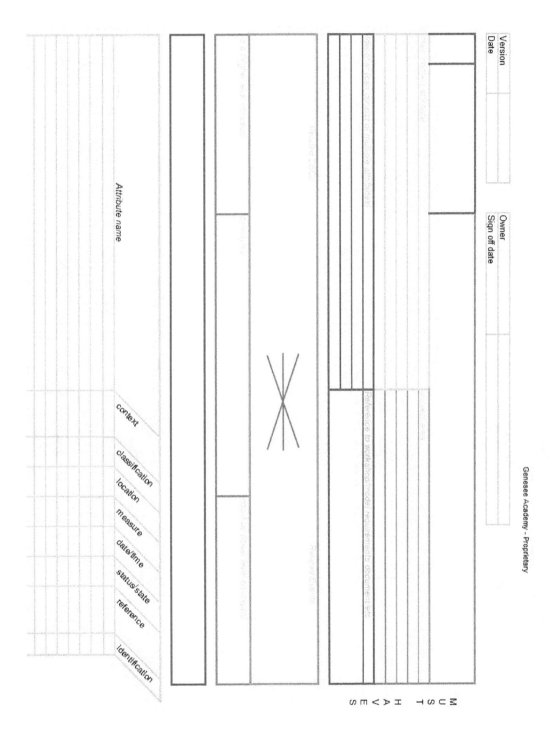

Event Canvas

Event

	Person	Place	Thing	Other Concept

NBR Matrix

Natural Business Relation (NBR)

CBC1

CBC2

CBC3

...

...

...

...

Version		Owner	
Date		Sign off date	
		Comes from workshop/e	

Name	Short description of the region

CBC1	CBC2	CBC3	CBC4	CBC5	CBC6	CBC7

CBC1	CBC2	CBC3	CBC4	CBC5	CBC6	CBC7

CBC1	CBC2	CBC3	CBC4	CBC5	CBC6	CBC7

Need Keyed Instance (Needs a describing	Y	N	Short description or actions to be taken after investigating the NBR - see Remarks next to example records

Descriptive information on NBR	List all possible descriptive information

About the Author

Remco Broekmans has 25+ years of experience working with all things data, including DW/BI, Data Modeling (Ensemble Modeling and Data Vault in particular), and Enterprise Integration. His professional focus is on aligning with the business side of organizations in ELM workshops and working with business people towards an Aligned, Refined, and Designed data model, a Logical Data Model fit for Data Vault or other Ensemble patterns.

Remco fulfills different roles as a data modeling professional, trainer, facilitator, coach, and advisor.

Remco is publishing articles on LinkedIn on various data modeling topics and is an integral part of the team developing course materials for the Data Vault Certification and the Business Mapping and ELM training. In the past, Remco has developed several education courses on Business Intelligence and Data Warehousing. He frequently speaks at conferences and DAMA meetings on various topics in data modeling, with a big connection to the Business-First philosophy of Enterprise Data Initiatives.

Index

www.ingramcontent.com/pod-product-compliance
Lightning Source LLC
Chambersburg PA
CBHW080543060326
40690CB00022B/5206